MEDIEVAL ESSEX
CHURCHES

Published by
THE ESSEX COUNTY COUNCIL. CHELMSFORD
ESSEX RECORD OFFICE PUBLICATIONS, No. 60
1972

Printed by
SILVER END PRESS
LETTERPRESS DIVISION OF E T HERON & CO LTD,
ESSEX AND LONDON

15p

SBN 900360 15 1

NAVESTOCK BELFRY

This magnificent timber-framed belfry was erected some time before 1250, and in 1297 contained two bells. It was placed at the south-west angle of the church and its erection immediately preceded that of the south aisle (see Plate 16). Shortage of good local building stone and the high cost of transporting stone from other counties, compelled Essex builders to turn to substitutes, first timber and later brick. The widespread use of timber led to the evolution of highly advanced and technically efficient joinery, and in Essex the heritage of timber-framed buildings is perhaps richer and more varied than in any other part of England. Of these buildings, the 65 belfries take pride of place. Most of them are fairly closely grouped in the southern half of the county, and each was individually designed. Some, like Navestock, Margaretting, Mundon, Magdalen Laver and Blackmore, are outside the west end of the church, while rather more, like Mountnessing, Horndon-on-the-Hill, Thundersley, Good Easter, Black Notley and Chipping Ongar have massive structures built within the western end of the nave. One, West Hanningfield, built on to the west end of the church probably in the first half of the fourteenth century, is unique, for its plan is cruciform.

INTRODUCTION

In 1956 the Essex Record Office published *Essex Churches 600–1800*, a picture booklet by Mr A. C. Edwards, then County History Adviser, to accompany the current exhibition at Ingatestone Hall. So popular did this subject prove that a reprint was necessary in August, and this had sold out early in 1957. Slightly revised editions by Mr Edwards were published in 1960 and 1966. The present booklet has been prepared in connection with the 1972 exhibition at Ingatestone Hall, 'The Medieval Church in Essex' and, like the exhibition, its terminal date of reference is the Reformation. Even so, the subject is an enormous one to condense into so few pages, and, after much consideration, it has been thought best to restrict the scope of the booklet to a pictorial study of the main parts of medieval churches and their furniture and fittings. This means that the history of the church as an institution, the evolution of the parish and the development of medieval ecclesiastical architecture, subjects of considerable interest and importance, treated in some detail in the exhibition, are limited to the confines of this introduction. The omission of religious houses is less regrettable for *Essex Monasteries*, a pictorial record of religious houses during the Middle Ages, published by the Essex Record Office in 1964, remains in print.

It is not known when Christianity first reached Essex and the earliest evidence of a Christian community is at Colchester during the third and fourth centuries. In the early Saxon period Christianity reached Essex from two sources—Roman and Celtic. When St Augustine came from Rome in 597 with a Christian mission to pagan England he soon converted King Ethelbert of Kent and his people. In 604 he sent his companion, Mellitus, to be bishop of London and to preach the gospel in the kingdom of the East Saxons. The king, Sabert, nephew of Ethelbert, became a Christian, but on his death the kingdom reverted to paganism and so remained until 653, when St Cedd, a monk of Lindisfarne in Northumbria, was sent with another priest to preach and to baptise in Essex. He built a monastery at Tilbury, and a church at Bradwell-juxta-Mare, and this is usually regarded as the real beginning of Christianity in Essex. In 664 Cedd died of plague after travelling north to attend the Synod of Whitby, which decided that England should follow the Roman, and not the Celtic practices of the church.

By the beginning of the seventh century the parish began to emerge as a local ecclesiastical unit in Northumbria and Kent, but, as Sir Frank Stenton pointed out, the general establishment of a parochial system was impossible until kings and their companions had been persuaded to build and endow churches on their estates, and the impulse to this work spread very gradually from the higher to the lower ranks of the nobility. In Essex during the later Saxon period the majority of churches and chapels were founded not by kings or bishops, but by lay noblemen, usually the lord of the manor. The founder of such a church regarded it as his property which would yield an income to him and his heirs, and the origin of lay patronage (possession of advowsons) in England lies in the custom which allowed the founder of a church to appoint its priest.

Despite a lack of documentary evidence and the general omission of churches from the Domesday Book, it is becoming increasingly clear from other sources, chiefly place-name and archaeological evidence, that the parochial system was well-established in Essex at the time of the Conquest, even if the parish boundaries were not always clearly defined, and that it was virtually fully developed by about 1200. The earliest extant contemporary list of churches, drawn up about 1254, includes some 380 churches, exclusive of chapels. By 1300 the number of churches had only increased to 397, while in addition there were 72 chapels. The siting of a church is itself of considerable interest; since most parish churches in the county originated as manorial churches they are usually close to the ancient manor house or its site, but a number of churches occupy even older sites, used originally for pagan worship. Indeed, it was Pope Gregory who advised St Augustine not to destroy the pagan places of worship, but to convert them into Christian churches, and at Thundersley the church of St Peter stands on a precipitous hill, the worshipping place of Thunor (see Plate 3).

At least fourteen Essex churches still have Saxon work in their fabric, and in some, like Hadstock, where the nave and north transept are intact, the work is extensive. With the exceptions of Bradwell-juxta-Mare, Prittlewell and Greensted-juxta-Ongar, the pre-Conquest work is probably all of the century preceding the Conquest and plans of buildings of this date are marked by an entire lack of care in setting out, the angles are seldom right angles, and the walls are always of rubble, generally about $2\frac{1}{2}$ feet thick. Norman churches ($c.1060–c.1190$) are unusually common in Essex, but in contrast the Early English period ($c.1190–c.1300$) is poorly represented; few new churches were erected and most work consisted of additions, mainly aisles, to existing structures. This is hardly surprising; as more churches were built fewer would be required, and the decree of Pope Innocent III (1198–1216) which provided that in future all tithe should be paid to the parish priest unless it was already being paid to some other recipient, undoubtedly stifled the desire of local lay lords to found new churches. There is some evidence of a recovery in building activity by the beginning of the fourteenth century, and during the short-lived Decorated period ($c.1300–c.1350$) work was produced of a richness and variety not generally met with in a parish church, as in the chancels at Fyfield and Lawford, and the south aisle at All Saints', Maldon. The wave of church rebuilding which roughly coincided with the opening of the Perpendicular period ($c.1340–c.1500$) gave East Anglia the great parish churches for which it is famous, but also spread into north Essex and resulted in the magnificent structures at Saffron Walden, Thaxted, Dedham, and Great Bromley.

ACKNOWLEDGMENTS
The valuable advice and suggestions of my colleagues at the Record Office have lightened the task of preparing this publication, and I wish to thank in particular Mr K. C. Newton, County and Hon. Diocesan Archivist, and Mr J. L. M. Booker, Senior Assistant Archivist. To Mr A. C. Edwards, MA, who retired from the post of County History Adviser in 1969, special thanks are due for giving so freely of his immense knowledge of Essex churches. Once again the County Visual and Aural Aids Service team has borne cheerfully the brunt of the photographic work by preparing the cover, frontispiece, and plates numbered 3, 5–7, 9, 11, 12, 14–16, 18–20, 22–27, 30–35, 37–39, 43–45. Mr N. Hammond, Senior Photographic Assistant in the Essex Record Office, provided the photographs for numbers 4, 10, 17, 40, 41, while numbers 13, 21, 28, 29, 36, 42 are taken from negatives in the large and valuable collection presented to the Record Office by Mr H. F. Hayllar. Numbers 1, 2 and 8 are from the photograph library of the Royal Commission on Historical Monuments (England) and are Crown Copyright. Finally, this booklet would not have been possible without the generous co-operation of the Clergy of Essex, to whom I extend my thanks.

J. R. SMITH

The cover illustration shows the fourteenth-century glass panel depicting the Virgin and Child in the parish church of St Mary and St Hugh, Harlow.

1. BRADWELL-JUXTA-MARE

In 653 Sigebert the Good, King of the pagan East Saxons and friend of the Christian king of Northumbria, was baptised by the bishop of Lindisfarne. In answer to his request for Christian teachers Cedd and another priest were sent to preach and baptise in Essex. The two centres of Cedd's work were Tilbury where a monastery was established, and Bradwell-juxta-Mare where the church of St Peter was built c.654. In the Middle Ages it was a chapel-of-ease to Bradwell, but was eventually desecrated and used as a lighthouse in the Tudor period, and later as a barn. It was restored and re-consecrated about 1920, shortly after this photograph was taken.

2. GREENSTED-JUXTA-ONGAR

Most churches in Saxon Essex were built of wood, but St Andrew's at Greensted-juxta-Ongar is the sole survivor. Without denying the tradition that it was the place where St Edmund's body rested on its journey from London to Bury St Edmunds in 1013 there is reason to doubt whether it was built in that year, for dendro-magnetic tests carried out in 1960 suggested a date of about 835 for most of the present nave, although some of the timbers were dated to an earlier building of the mid-seventh century. Its isolated position next to the old manor house suggests that it may have been founded by the local Saxon lord. It is the oldest wooden church in England and probably the world.

3. THUNDERSLEY

When Pope Gregory sent his Christian mission to England in 597 he advised Augustine not to destroy the pagan places of worship, but to convert them into Christian churches by washing the walls with holy water, erecting altars, and substituting holy relics and symbols for the images of pagan gods. Of the early Essex churches erected on pagan sites perhaps the best known is St Peter, Thundersley, which stands on a precipitous hill, the worshipping place of Thunor, the thunder-god, the most honoured of all gods among the Saxon peoples. The oldest part of the present church is the nave and north and south aisles, built early in the thirteenth century. The timber-framed belfry was added about two centuries later. In 1965 the old chancel was demolished and the church extended 45 feet to the east, a response to the expanding dormitory population of the parish.

4. CONSECRATION CROSSES

For the consecration of a church twelve crosses were carved, painted or depicted on the fabric, outside and inside the walls of the church. They were anointed with holy oil by the bishop and were lit with candles on the anniversary of consecration. Normally these crosses were about seven or eight feet above ground to prevent passers-by brushing against them. The bishop used a short ladder to reach them. The two crosses in this picture flank the niche beneath the east window of Great Sampford church. They date from about 1325.

5–7. BUILDING MATERIALS

Essex churches display an ingenious use of inferior materials, for there is no good building stone in the county. At Sandon, Tudor masons built the handsome red-brick porch and tower using blue vitreous bricks to form a pattern of saltires in honour of St Andrew, the patron saint of the church. For the fabric of the nave and chancel, the Norman masons used a mixture of flints, pebbles, indurated gravel and Roman brick and tile, reserving the most perfect Roman bricks for the quoins. At least 103 Essex churches have re-used Roman material in their structure.

8. DOORS AND DOORWAYS

Most churches had a north and south door to the nave, and some a west door as well. The north door was known as the Devil's door and was left open at baptismal services so that evil spirits thought to be in a child could, when it was christened, pass from the child through the doorway. This door was also used for the ceremonially important processions; the procession passed through it, into the churchyard and round the east end of the church, and in again by the south door. Saxon doors and doorways were usually quite plain but from the Norman period south doors in particular were decorated and often became objects of some beauty, perhaps a result of Christ's famous words, 'I am the door: by me if any man enter he shall be saved'. North doors and doorways generally remained plain, unless the manor house or village stood on that side of the church, and many were blocked after the Reformation. The illustration shows the south door of c.1260 at Bocking with elaborate scrolled and foliated ironwork thought to be the work of the famous smith Thomas of Leighton. The fourteenth-century doorway was restored in the last century.

9. PORCH

By the end of the Middle Ages most churches had a porch on the south side, or on the north side if the manor house lay on that side, and a few had porches on both sides. They were still unusual in the thirteenth century, but from about 1300 they began to be regarded as a necessity and played an important role in church ceremony. It was here that penitents received absolution before entering the church, those breaking vows did penance, while those breaking marriage vows stood wrapped in a white sheet. Women knelt here to be 'churched' after the birth of a child, and part of the marriage service was held here and the ring placed on the finger; civil business was conducted, executors of wills made payment of legacies, and coroners sometimes held their courts in the porch. It was one of the 'stations' during processions and protected the door from inclement weather. Thirteen porches dating from the fourteenth century survive in Essex. Perhaps the earliest and certainly one of the finest, is the south porch at Aldham, built about 1325.

10. PRIEST'S DOOR

The chancel and sanctuary were the special responsibility of the parish priest and he had his own entrance. It was also useful at night when he had to enter to obtain the necessary articles if called upon to visit the sick or dying. The door shown here is in the south side of the Norman apse of St Mary Magdalene, East Ham.

11. Font

Fonts are generally in a prominent place, often immediately west of the south doorway or at the west end of the nave; this is appropriate, for it is here that life as a Christian begins. In the Middle Ages the baptismal service began outside the door, in the porch if there was one, and finished at the font. Early fonts, in which adults stood while the baptismal water was poured over them, were tub-shaped. Later, the baptised were chiefly children; they were completely immersed and the font was often raised on a low stand for convenience. When, later still, it became customary to pour water over the child, bowls were made smaller and raised higher on pillars or pedestals. Many bowls are therefore of an earlier date than the base on which they stand. Within this framework the design and decoration were usually suggested by the prevailing style of architecture, and the octagonal fifteenth-century font at Belchamp St Paul is typical of its period.

12. Font Cover

In 1236 Archbishop Rich of Canterbury decreed that locked covers should be fitted to fonts to prevent the hallowed water being stolen and put to superstitious uses. The earliest form of cover was a flat wooden lid which was lifted off during baptismal services, but in the fifteenth century it developed into a canopy, often of splendid and massive proportions, occasionally completely enclosing the font. In the cover at Littlebury, shown here, which dates from about 1500, two of the panels are opened when the font is in use.

13. NAVE

The nave is the part of the church which accommodates the congregation during services. Most early churches comprised only a nave and sanctuary in which stood the altar, but as congregations grew larger, aisles were often added. In the absence of generally recognisable architectural details, such as windows and doorways, Saxon naves are distinguishable by a lack of care in setting out and angles which are seldom square, while Norman naves are recognisable by their proportions which were nearly always two squares; in other words, the length was double the width. Before the Reformation the nave was also used for parish meetings, religious plays, church sales, dancing, and other merrymaking associated with the main festivals. The illustration shows the Norman nave at Stanford Rivers; the timber-framed bell turret and crown post roof are of the fifteenth century.

14. SANCTUARY

The sanctuary is in the easternmost part of a church and accommodates the high altar. It has always, as the name suggests, been the most sacred part of the church and during services is occupied exclusively by those who minister in the services of the altar. Early east-ends were either square or apsidal, and there is now little evidence as to which termination was most popular, as in the great majority of cases the east end has been entirely rebuilt. At Copford the twelfth-century apsidal sanctuary contains magnificent wall-painting of c.1140, including Christ enthroned inside the complete circle of a rainbow held aloft by angels. On the great arch spanning the entrance are displayed the signs of the zodiac.

15. CHANCEL

The chancel is at the eastern end of the church between the nave and sanctuary and is used principally by the choir and sometimes by deacons and servers assisting the priest in the service. Its name derives from the Latin *cancellus*, a screen, which in the Middle Ages separated the chancel from the nave. The illustration shows the Norman chancel, with apsidal sanctuary beyond, at St Mary Magdalene, East Ham.

16. AISLE

In most cases the first addition to an early church was an aisle; they were built to accommodate more altars, larger congregations, and to provide paths for processions. Many aisles were built in the thirteenth century, like that on the south side at Navestock, shown here, which dates from about 1250. The arcade, excluding the contemporary south chapel, is of four bays of rough timber construction, cleverly and effectively disguised by contemporary plaster, imitating stonework.

17. TOWER

The tower was an important part of the medieval parish church; its chief, and in the later Middle Ages its only, purpose was to house the bells. In Saxon churches of the eleventh century the main entrance was a doorway in the west wall of the nave, and where there was a west tower, as at Little Bardfield, shown here, the ground floor was utilised as a porch. Many early churches in Essex were built without towers, and bell-cotes, of sufficient size to hold one or two bells, were constructed on the east or west gable of the nave.

18. BELLS

In the later Middle Ages bells were rung far more frequently than today. They summoned parishioners to worship and were rung at festivals, baptisms, marriages and funerals. They were rung during storms and tempests in the belief that nature could be calmed, and they were rung if fire, flood or other disaster threatened the parish. And when Queen Margaret visited Saffron Walden in 1444, the churchwardens paid men 4d for 'ryngyng wanne ye quene was her'. At Margaretting the early fifteenth-century timber-framed belfry contains the only complete ring of four pre-Reformation bells in the county, and, happily, they are still in frequent use. This one, the tenor, was made about 1420 by John Walgrave.

19. CHANTRY

Chantries were endowments for maintaining priests to say masses for the souls of the founder and others named by him, and the development of the plan of some Essex churches owes much to the chantry cult which became popular after about 1300. Chapels were sometimes provided for the use of the chantry, and they would often contain the tombs of the founder and members of his family. The chapel shown here is in All Saints', Maldon. It was built on to the east end of the south aisle about 1443 by Sir Robert D'Arcy (1385–1448) to house 'Darcyeschaunterye' which was to be set up by his executors after his death, and was to have two chaplains who were to celebrate divine service daily. The 'Decorated' east window is contemporary with the building of the south aisle (c.1330), but was re-set when the chapel was built and the old east wall became redundant.

20. ANCHORITE

Anchorites and anchoresses were persons desirous of living pious lives. They were conducted in a ritual procession to the cell in which they would spend the remainder of their lives, and the door was blocked up and sealed. One small window admitted light and food; another gave a view of the high altar. Few cells remain in England, none in Essex. At East Ham, on the north side of the chancel, there remains the blocked doorway and tiny interior window of a cell, probably constructed about 1500. Anchorites were buried beneath the cell, and the remains of two were found when the area of the East Ham cell was excavated in 1931.

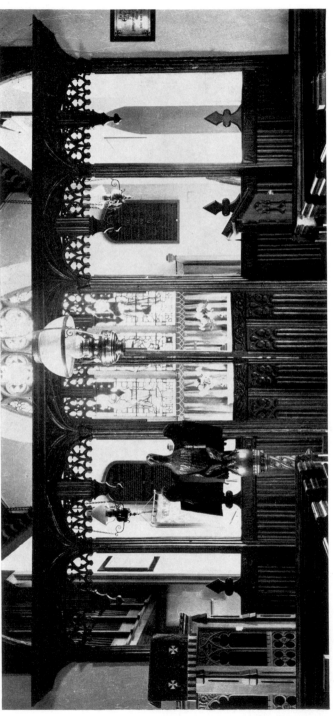

21. SCREEN AND ROOD LOFT

The medieval church was in two parts: at the east end the chancel and sanctuary were the preserve of the parish priest, while the nave, aisles and transepts were the province of the parishioners. The two parts were separated by a rood screen, so named from the rood (a carved figure of Christ crucified and attendant figures of the Virgin and St John) placed above the screen. Many screens were surmounted by a gallery or loft which enabled the rood lights to be attended during services. Generally, the loft was about six feet deep, the floor projecting beyond the screen back and front. In 1561 it was ordered that rood lofts were to be destroyed, but not the screens, and it was during the eighteenth and nineteenth centuries that most of the latter were recklessly swept away. Nevertheless, Essex can be proud of its surviving medieval screens; they enrich the interior of about 55 parish churches and are witness to the consummate skill of medieval carpenters and woodcarvers. One of the most delightful is at North Weald, erected about 1500, which is unique in Essex for having preserved the under-coving of the rood loft.

22. ROOD LOFT STAIRWAY

Access to the rood loft was either by ladder in humble churches, or by narrow stairways. Many stairways survive; their positions vary considerably but the most common are in the north wall of the nave where there is no aisle, or in the angle between the chancel arch and the arcade where there is an aisle. The staircase at Little Baddow was cut into the north wall of the nave during the later Middle Ages, possibly at the same time as the chancel was rebuilt in the middle of the fourteenth century.

23. SQUINT

In order to give the congregation sitting in the aisles or transepts a view of the sanctuary during Mass, openings known as 'squints' or 'hagioscopes' were cut at an angle through the wall at the side of the chancel arch. The illustration shows an early fourteenth-century 'squint' cut through the wall north of the chancel arch at Danbury.

24. STONE ALTAR

In 1076 Archbishop Lanfranc issued an edict that all altars should be made of stone. Most had five carved crosses (one at each corner and one in the middle) representing the five wounds of Christ. At the Reformation nearly all stone altars were destroyed; at Great Hallingbury, about 1550, two men were paid three shillings 'for taking down the altars and carrying away the rubbish'. In some parishes the old altar slabs have been found, and in a few, as at Chickney, they have been restored to their original use.

25. STOUP

Just inside the church, close to the door, or outside in the porch, was a small niche with a stone basin formed in the wall, as a receptacle for holy water, blessed every Sunday. All who entered the church dipped a finger in and made the sign of the cross on their forehead and breast to remind them of their baptismal vows and the need of cleansing from sin. The illustration shows the fifteenth-century stoup at Danbury, inside the north (and main) door.

26. CRESSET STONE

The cresset was a stone slab with cup-like hollows which were filled with oil and floating wicks to provide light for persons performing night duties in the church. They are extremely rare, and the one at Blackmore is the only example in Essex.

27. REREDOS

The wall behind an altar was usually ornamented with panelling and was often enriched with a profusion of niches, buttresses, pinnacles, images and other decorations, painted in brilliant colours. Like the altar in front of it, the reredos suffered severely at the Reformation and few medieval examples remain in the county. The best preserved is in the north transept at Thaxted; the six buttressed and crocketed niches, which originally housed images, are richly canopied, and in the cornice along the top is a carved head of Christ flanked by angels. It is made of plaster and is probably contemporary with the building of the transept in about 1400.

28. Sedilia

The name sedilia, Latin for seats, is applied by way of distinction to the seats on the south side of the sanctuary. Here, while the Creed and *Gloria* were sung, the priest and his attendants could take a short rest in the long ceremony of Mass. They are generally recessed in the wall like niches and usually contain three separate seats. Numerous good medieval examples remain, and that at Fyfield, shown here, dates from the rebuilding of the chancel, about 1325.

29. Piscina

In the ninth century Pope Leo IV decreed that a drain for the disposal of water in which sacred vessels were washed during Mass should be made near every altar, and in its earliest form the piscina was a drainhole in the pavement. In Norman churches pillar-piscinas, stone shafts supporting a basin from which the water drained down a vertical boring, were fairly common. From about the middle of the twelfth century the basin began to be placed in a niche in the south wall of the sanctuary with a drain hole running through the wall to the ground outside. During the thirteenth century double piscinas became popular; one basin was used for washing the chalice and the other for washing the priest's hands. The earliest Essex example of this type is at Barnston, and dates from about 1200.

30. EASTER SEPULCHRE

The Easter Sepulchre, a representation of the entombment of Christ, was set up at Easter on the north side of the sanctuary or chancel. It was usually a temporary wooden erection, but canopied tombs in the north wall, previously designed to be a sepulchre, were also used. On Good Friday the Sacrament was placed in a small receptacle and laid in the sepulchre where it was continuously watched until the early hours of Easter Sunday, when it was returned to the High Altar. From about the beginning of the fourteenth century stone sepulchres were specially designed for the sole purpose of enshrining the Sacrament. They are rare in Essex, and the best example, dating from the end of the fourteenth century, is at Southchurch. Beneath the sepulchre is a tomb recess of slightly earlier date.

31. PULPIT

Pulpits began to be introduced into churches in the fourteenth century but examples of this period are rare, and there are none in Essex. In the fifteenth century preaching became general, and seven oak pulpits of this date have survived in the county; they are all octagonal and supported by conical stems, and most have enriched panelling, like this fine late fifteenth-century example at Leaden Roothing. The pulpit was normally placed on one side of the nave near the rood screen, and the clergy and others who occupied the chancel during Mass proceeded into the nave to hear the sermon.

32. Lectern

The lectern is now to be found at the west end of the nave and is used to hold the Bible from which the Lessons are read. From the early fourteenth century, the date of the oldest known example, until the Reformation, it stood in the middle of the chancel and was moved to a position north of the High Altar for the chanting of the Gospel during Mass. Many medieval lecterns were made of brass in the form of an eagle with wings extended to receive the Bible, but in Essex most were of wood, like this fifteenth-century example at Newport, which has a double desk with sloping sides, supported by an octagonal standard with trefoil-headed panels.

33. Wall Painting

Before the Reformation almost every square foot of wall-space in a church was occupied by paintings, either of an ornamental character or illustrating miracles, legends and doctrines of the Church. Favourite subjects included St Christopher on the wall facing the main door, and the 'Doom' or 'Day of Judgement' over the chancel arch. During and after the Reformation they were covered with whitewash, but over the past century a surprising number have been discovered and once more revealed for our admiration, like this fragment of a delightful fourteenth-century St Christopher and Christ Child discovered at Lambourne in 1951.

34. GLASS

Medieval glass added glorious colour to the churches of Essex, but little survived the fury of the zealots after the Reformation. In 1559, the Heybridge churchwardens paid John Harrode 4d 'for blotting out the images of the glass windows'. One of the earliest and most delightful surviving fragments is this late thirteenth-century crowned figure of St Helen with staff and book in the east window of the chancel at North Ockenden.

35. CHEST

There are about 40 pre-Reformation parish chests in Essex, ranging in date from the twelfth to the early sixteenth century. During the Middle Ages they were important items of furniture, and in them were kept the parishioners' wills, the accounts of the churchwardens and the rich vestments used for church services and processions. The earliest chests were roughly hewn from a single tree-trunk and are termed 'dug-outs'; there are fourteen in Essex. Later the chests were made out of thick planks and bound with iron, like this fourteenth-century example at Copford.

36. Poor Box

The giving of alms has always been considered a Christian virtue, but before the Reformation, when there was no public responsibility for poverty, it was also an individual Christian's duty. Medieval poor boxes were generally made from roughly hollowed pieces of tree trunks with iron bands to strengthen them, and three survive in Essex from this period, at Canewdon, Runwell and Steeple Bumpstead. The finest is undoubtedly that at Steeple Bumpstead; it has three locks, stands on a panelled octagonal pedestal, and dates from about 1500.

37. Banner and Stave Lockers

Before the Reformation, processions in and around the church formed an important part of the services on Sundays and Feast Days. For these processions, banners on staves and processional crosses on tall shafts were used. In many churches lockers were provided at the west end of the nave for the staves and processional crosses; they were usually seven to twelve feet in height, about eighteen inches wide and about twelve inches deep. While some of these cupboards remain, few retain their original oak doors. In Essex the only two examples are in Chelmsford Cathedral. They date from the late fifteenth century and still possess their original doors.

38. Misericord

On each side of the chancel were stalls for the priests and choristers; the earliest surviving examples date from the beginning of the fourteenth century, but it is clear that they were in use at an earlier date. Some stalls had small hinged tip-up seats, on the underside of which was a projecting ledge (the misericord) which gave support to the aged and infirm during the long period of standing in medieval services. These seats often had carvings, known as 'baberies', on the undersides, and from the surviving examples it is evident that the woodcarvers were free to give full play to their imagination, as did the late fourteenth-century carver of the fox with distaff, lion's head, and wolf carrying off a monk, at Castle Hedingham. Misericords are rare in Essex, and the only examples are at Castle Hedingham and Belchamp St Paul.

39. Benches

Benches, or seats in the nave for the congregation, began to be introduced into churches early in the fourteenth century, and by the beginning of the sixteenth century most churches were furnished with them. Where they were not provided it was customary for the worshippers to stand during services, when they were not on their knees. The earliest benches had solid ends and were devoid of ornament, but in the fifteenth century, the golden age of woodworkers, bench ends were often richly decorated with carving. The tops of some ends were finished with a carved decoration known as a 'poppy-head', from the French word poupée (puppet or figure-head), like this fifteenth-century bearded dog at Danbury. Other popular forms were human figures and grotesque heads.

40. STONE COFFIN

In the Middle Ages only the wealthy were buried in coffins; most people were laid in a grave wrapped in a woollen sheet and covered with earth. Medieval coffins were always of stone, and in the twelfth and thirteenth centuries the lid usually bore the form of a cross, either incised or in relief. A few complete stone coffins remain in Essex; although badly weathered, this example at Great Bardfield remains almost intact, and has recently been taken into the church for better preservation.

41. LYCH GATE

Lych was the old English word for a corpse. At the lych-gate the coffin was laid on a table while the priest said part of the burial service. Since only wealthy people were buried in coffins in the Middle Ages, most corpses were laid in a wooden parish coffin in which they were transported to the graveside where they were taken out and wrapped in a woollen sheet for burial. Two pre-Reformation lych-gates remain in Essex, at Finchingfield (shown here) and at Felsted; both were built about 1500.

42. BIER

Coffined burials remained the exception until the eighteenth-century, and it was customary for every parish to possess a bier and a coffin or shell to rest upon it, for carrying corpses to the graveyard. A few parishes still possess their old biers, but only the fifteenth-century example in Ridgwell church, shown here, is of pre-Reformation date. It is constructed of oak and has telescopic handles. The four octagonal legs have small capitals as do the braces.

43. WOOD EFFIGIES

Medieval effigies of deceased persons are common in churches throughout England. They are usually life-size, but are not necessarily portraits: in fact most effigies represent the deceased in the prime of life. The rich and varied range of monuments in Essex churches includes ten of a rare type, the oaken effigy, spanning the period c.1250–c.1350. The early fourteenth-century pair at Little Baddow are particularly interesting, and Dr Nikolaus Pevsner has described the woman in her exquisitely draped dress as being 'of uncommonly fine quality'.

44. BRASS

Monumental brasses are thin pieces of metal (an alloy of copper and zinc) with incised lines, let flush into a stone. They were introduced late in the thirteenth century and the chief centre of manufacture was always London. This delightful but sad little emblem of early mortality was engraved in memory of Thomas Heron, son and heir of Sir John Heron of Aldersbrook in Little Ilford, who died aged 14 years on 18th March 1517. He is shown with long hair and clothed in the long, wide-sleeved gown of the period. From his girdle hang an ink-horn and pen case. It is the sole figure of its kind in Essex, and is one of only two brasses representing school-boys in England.

45. CHARNEL

Many of the so-called crypts beneath medieval parish churches were nothing more than charnel houses or bone-holes. After centuries of burials the graveyard often became full of uncoffined remains, particularly in towns where there was no room to expand, and there was no alternative but to bury the dead on top of others. When a previous internment was disturbed the bones were deposited in the charnel. Similarly, the charnel housed the bones removed when extensions were made to the church, as at All Saints' Maldon where it was built beneath the new south aisle, erected about 1330.